Write the missing letter to finish each word.
Use

a   or   o

Well Done!
Well Done!

m ___ p

d ___ g

c ___ t

v ___ n

Bob Bug

Tips for reading Bob Bug together

This story practises these sounds:

r l _ _ _ _ u s
m c t g p a o

Ask your child to point to each of these letters and say the sound (e.g. *u* as in *umbrella*, not the letter name *yoo*). Look out for these letters in the story.

Before you begin, ask your child to read the title on page 17 by sounding out and blending. Look at the picture together. What do you think this story is about?

Remind your child to read unfamiliar words by saying the individual sounds and then blending them together quickly to read the word.

When you have finished reading the story, look through it again and:

- Ask your child, *Do you think there really was a rat in Bob Bug's bedroom? How do you know?*

- Find the words that begin with the *b* sound (*Bob, Bug, big, bad*). Does the *b* sound look the same in all of these words? Talk about capital letters and how they are used for names and at the beginning of sentences. Find some more words that begin with capital letters (*Mum, Dad*). Ask your child, *What sound does the capital letter make in these words?*

Bob is a bug.

Bob Bug has a mum. His mum is big.

Bob has a dad. His dad is fit.

Bob has a cup. It has a lid.

Bob has a cot. His cot has a rug.

Bob Bug has a hug.

Activities

Write the first letter to finish these rhyming words.
Use

j   b   h   m

___ ug

___ ug

___ ug

___ ug

27

Write the first letter to finish these rhyming words. Use

h   r   b   c

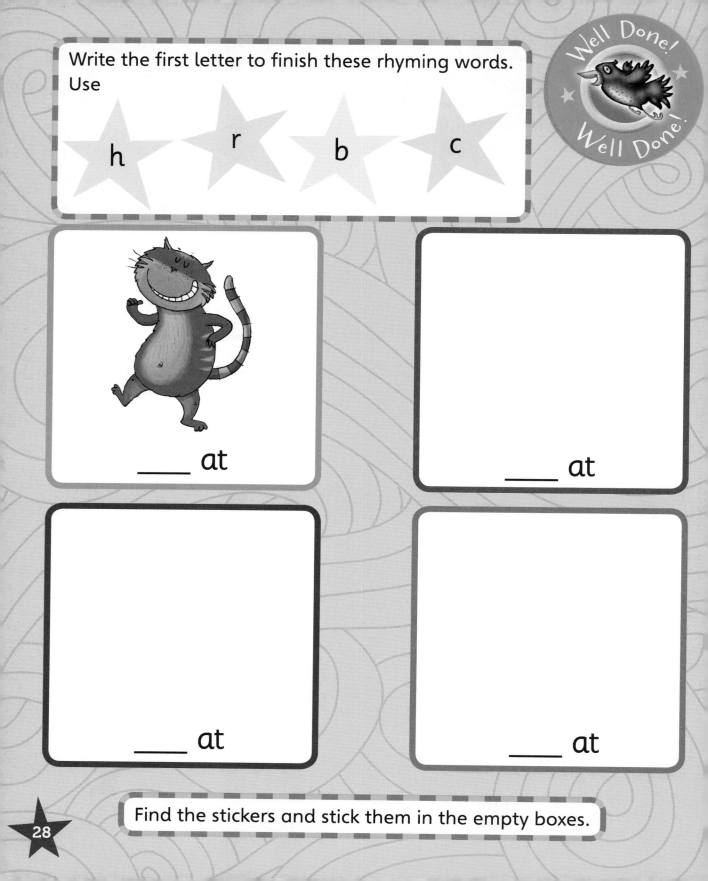

____ at

____ at

____ at

____ at

Find the stickers and stick them in the empty boxes.

28

Dig, Dig, Dig!

Tips for reading Dig, Dig, Dig together

This story practises these sounds:

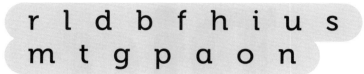

r l d b f h i u s
m t g p a o n

Ask your child to point to each of these letters and say the sound (e.g. *r* as in *rabbit*, not the letter name *ar*). Look out for these letters in the story.

Your child might find this word tricky:

of

Explain that this word is common, but the *f* in *of* is unusual and makes the *v* sound. Say the word for your child if they do not know it.

Before you begin, ask your child to read the title on page 29 by sounding out and blending. Look at the picture together. What do you think this story is about?

Remind your child to read unfamiliar words by saying the individual sounds and then blending them together quickly to read the word.

When you have finished reading the story, look through it again and:

- Talk about Tim and the dog on the last page, are they disappointed? Ask your child, *What did Tim think would be inside the tin?*
- Find the words that begin with the *l* sound (*lot, lid, lots*). Point to the middle letter in *lid* and ask your child, *What sound does this letter make?* Find more words with the *i* sound in the middle (*dig, Tim, his, big*). Have fun thinking of some other words with the *i* sound in the middle (*wig, him, bin, fit*).

Dig, dig, dig!
Tim and his dog had fun.

Dig, dig, dig!
Tim dug up a lot of mud.

Dig, dig, dig!
His dog dug up a rag.

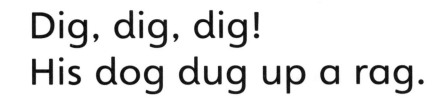

Dig, dig, dig!
Tim dug up a bus.

Dig, dig, dig!
A lid!

Dig, dig, dig!
A big tin!

And in it. . .

lots of bugs!

Activities

Circle the right word to finish each sentence.

Tim dug up a lot of _____ .

mud

bud

His dog dug up a _____ .

wag

rag

Tim dug up a _____ .

but

bus

He dug up a big _____ .

tin

bin

Read the sentences. Then colour the pictures.

Zak and the Vet

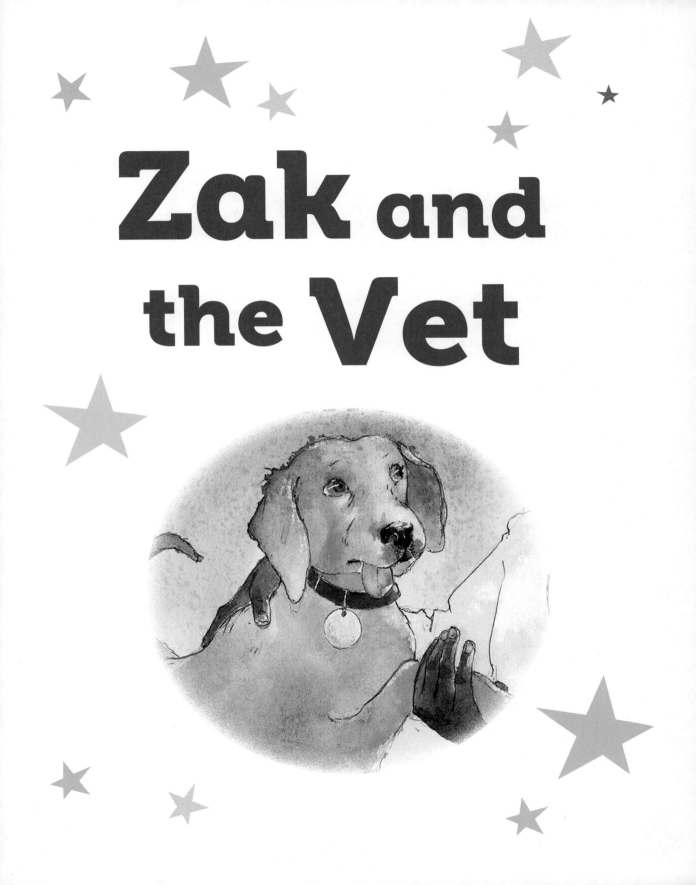

Tips for reading Zak and the Vet together

This story practises these sounds:

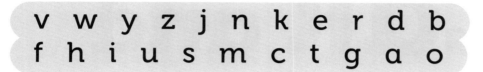

v w y z j n k e r d b
f h i u s m c t g a o

Ask your child to point to each of these letters and say the sound (e.g. *v* as in *van*, not the letter name *vee*). Look out for these letters in the story.

Your child might find these words tricky:

better   he   the   to   will

These words are common, but your child may not have learned how to sound them out yet. Say the words for your child if they do not know them.

Before you begin, ask your child to read the title on page 41 by sounding out and blending. Look at the picture together. What do you think this story is about?

Remind your child to read unfamiliar words by saying the individual sounds and then blending them together quickly to read the word.

When you have finished reading the story, look through it again and:

● Ask your child, *Who helped Zak?* Talk about what a vet is.

● Find the words that begin with the *v* sound (*van*, *vet*). Point to the *e* in *vet*. What sound does this make? Find some other words in the story with *e* in the middle (*red*, *Jen*, *get*, *yes*).

Zak did not sit. Zak ran.

Zak ran and ran!

Zak ran in the fog.
A red van hit him.

Jen and Zak went to the vet.

Zak had a bad cut. He had to get a jab.

Stickers for page 28

Sticker for page 63

Stickers for page 90

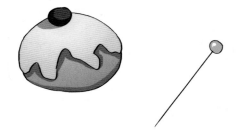

Sticker for page 95

Stickers for page 96

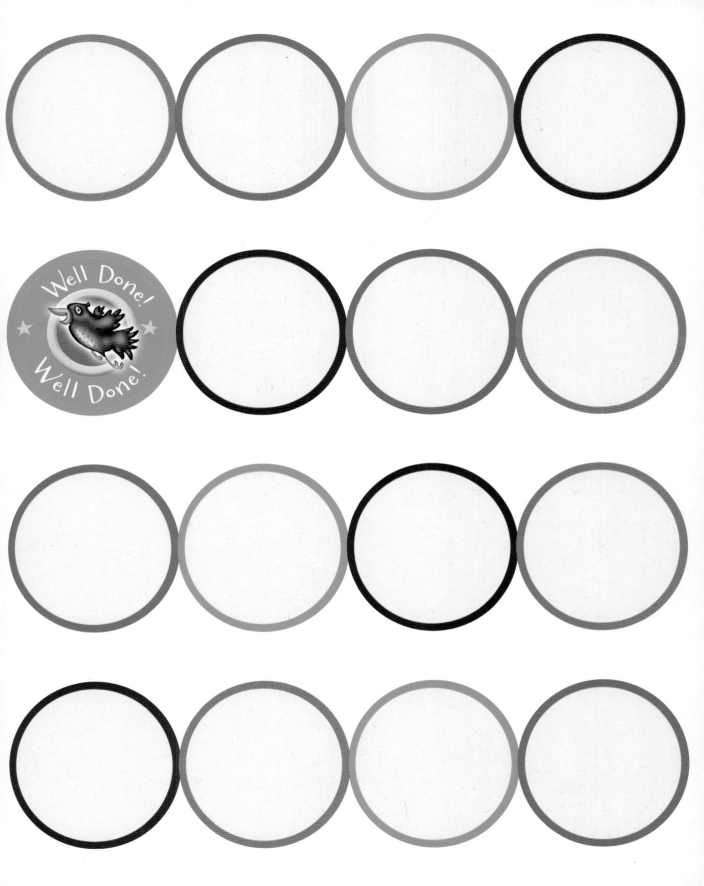

Zak did get better.

wag wag wag

Activities

Circle the right word to finish each sentence.

Zak did _____ sit.

hot

not

Zak ran and _____ !

ran

fan

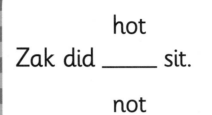

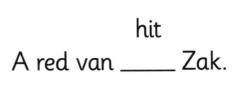

A red van _____ Zak.

hit

bit

Jen and Zak went to the _____ .

set

vet

Zak had a _____ cut.

bad

dad

lid

Zak _____ get better.

did

Well Done!
Well Done!

Mum Bug's Bag

Tips for reading Mum Bug's Bag together

This story practises these sounds:

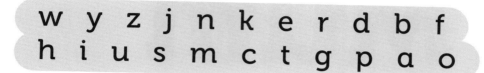

w y z j n k e r d b f
h i u s m c t g p a o

Ask your child to point to each of these letters and say the sound (e.g. *j* as in *jug*, not the letter name *jay*). Look out for these letters in the story.

Your child might find these words tricky:

her of the hole

These words are common, but your child may not have learned how to sound them out yet. Say the words for your child if they do not know them.

Before you begin, ask your child to read the title on page 53 by sounding out and blending. Look at the picture together. What do you think this story is about?

Remind your child to read unfamiliar words by saying the individual sounds and then blending them together quickly to read the word.

When you have finished reading the story, look through it again and:

- Ask your child, *What fell out of Mum Bug's bag?*
- Find the words that end with the *n* sound (*can, pen, fan, bun*). Notice the *u* in *bun*. Find other words in the story with the *u* sound in the middle (*Mum, Yuk, bug*). Have fun thinking of some other words with the *u* sound in the middle (*hum, hug, rug, run*).

Mum Bug has a red bag.
The bag has a zip.

Mum can fit a pen in her bag.

Mum can fit a pen and
a fan in her bag.

Mum can fit a pen and
a fan and
a bun in her bag.

Mum can fit a pen and
a fan and
a bun and
a pot of jam in her bag.

Mum has a hole in her bag!

The pen and
the fan and
the bun and
the jam get wet.

Mum Bug gets a big bag.

Activities

Circle the right word to finish each sentence.

Mum Bug has a red _____ .

bat

bag

Mum can fit a _____ in her bag.

pet

pen

bus
Mum Bug can fit a ____ in her bag.
bun

big
Mum Bug gets a ____ bag.
bit

Read the sentences. Then find the sticker to finish the picture on page 63.

Cat Naps

Tips for reading Cat Naps together

This story practises these sounds:

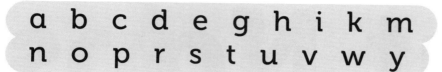

a b c d e g h i k m
n o p r s t u v w y

Ask your child to point to each of these letters and say the sound (e.g. *b* as in *bug*, not the letter name *bee*). Look out for these letters in the story.

Your child might find these words tricky:

of and it's

These words are common, but your child may not have learned how to sound them out yet. Say the words for your child if they do not know them.

Before you begin, ask your child to read the title on page 65 by sounding out and blending. Look at the picture together. What do you think this story is about?

Remind your child to read unfamiliar words by saying the individual sounds and then blending them together quickly to read the word.

When you have finished reading the story, look through it again and:

- Talk about what Kit Cat might be thinking on page 70.
- Find the words that end with the *p* sound (*top, nap, cap*). Notice that *cap* and *nap* sound the same at the end because they rhyme. Have fun thinking of some other words that rhyme with *nap* and *cap* (*tap, map, lap, gap*).

Top Cat had a nap in a cap.

Kit Cat had a nap in a sun hat.

Top Cat had a nap in a big top hat.

Kit Cat had a nap on a mat.
Top Cat had a nap on a rug.

Kit Cat had a nap in a cot.
Top Cat had a nap on a bed.

Pad pad pad! Wag wag wag!
Yap yap yap!

It's a dog! Run, Top Cat!
Run, Kit Cat!

Top Cat and Kit Cat had a nap on top of a van.

Activities

Circle the right word to finish each sentence.

tap

Top Cat had a nap in a _____ .

cap

hat

Top Cat had a nap in a big top _____ .

sat

75

Top Cat had a nap on a _____ .

rug

hug

Top Cat had a nap on _____ of a van.

mop

top

Read the sentences. Then colour the pictures.

The
Big Cod

Tips for reading The Big Cod together

This story practises these sounds:

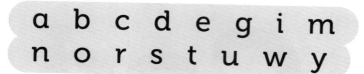

a b c d e g i m
n o r s t u w y

Ask your child to point to each of these letters and say the sound (e.g. *d* as in *dog*, not the letter name *dee*). Look out for these letters in the story.

Your child might find these words tricky:

the and Tim's

These words are common, but your child may not have learned how to sound them out yet. Say the words for your child if they do not know them.

Before you begin, ask your child to read the title on page 77 by sounding out and blending. Look at the picture together. What do you think this story is about?

Remind your child to read unfamiliar words by saying the individual sounds and then blending them together quickly to read the word.

When you have finished reading the story, look through it again and:

- Talk about if you would rather use a fishing net or a fishing rod and why.

- Find some words in the story that end with the *t* sound (*net, sit, it, bit, wet*). Read each word by sounding out and blending. Which of these words rhyme? Think of other words that rhyme with *net* and *wet* (*bet, get, jet, let, met, pet, set, vet*).

Tim has a net and a can.

Tim's Dad has a rod and a can.

Tim and Dad sit and sit.

Dad tugs and tugs.

The cod tugs and tugs.

Dad gets wet.

Activities

Circle the right word to
finish each sentence.

net

Tim has a _____ and a can.

wet

nod

Tim's Dad has a _____ and a can.

rod

87

The ___ tugs and tugs.

cod

pod

Dad gets ___ .

vet

wet

Read the sentences. Then colour the pictures.

Phonics fun!

Spot the odd one out

On each bus, find and colour two pictures that begin with the letter on the bus. Then find a sticker that also begins with that letter and stick it on the bus.

Well Done! Well Done!

b

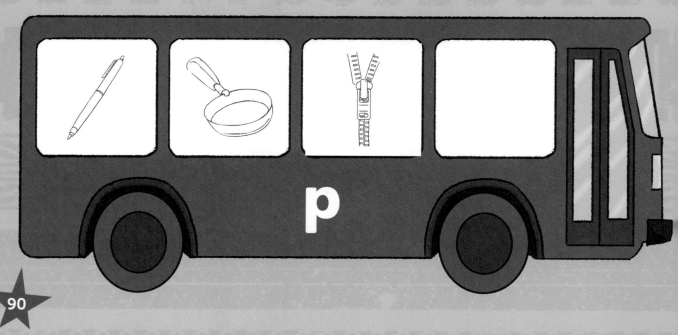

p

I spy...

Read the words. Write over each word when you have found the matching picture. Match the word to the right picture. Then colour the pictures.

tap  rat 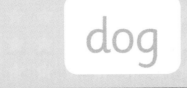 dog

hen mop cat

91

Missing letters

The words on each rug rhyme. Write the missing letter to finish each word.
Use

i   or   **o**

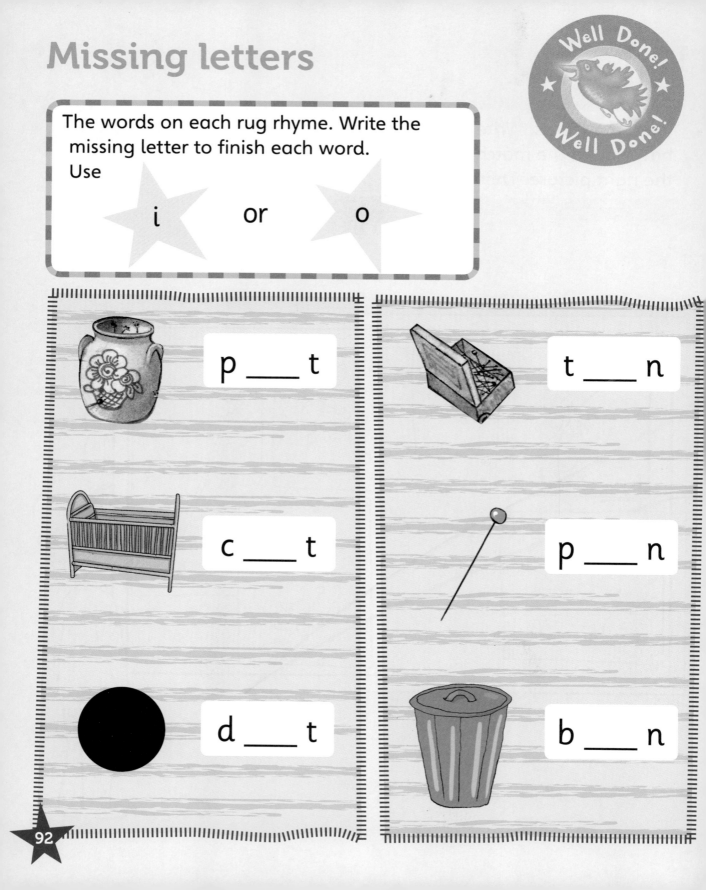

p __ t

c __ t

d __ t

t __ n

p __ n

b __ n

Word search

Read the words in grey and find them in the word search.
Write over each word when you have found it.

cut	mix	big	yum	tip
rub	lot	but	got	yes

```
r    u    b    y    c
y    m    i    x    u
u    i    g    o    t
m    y    e    s    i
b    u    t    e    p
y    l    o    t    g
```

93

Mix up some rhymes

Choose four colours. Colour the things that rhyme in the same colour.

Well Done!
Well Done!

log

sun

rat

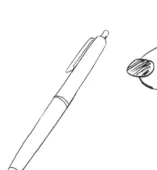

pen

dog

bun

cat

hen

Balloon game

Throw a dice. What number do you get?

Find the balloon with the number on it. Colour the balloon if you can read the word.

Play until you have coloured all the balloons.

hen
1

rat
2

dog
3

bus
4

zip
5

jam
6

Then find the sticker to finish the picture.

Get Bob Bug home!

Play this game with a friend.
You will need a counter each and one dice.
Start at the shop. Take turns to throw the dice and move your counters along the track to get home.
Read the word you land on or miss a go!

cat   pen   tin   bun   dog   fan

hit

bus   ran   wet   log   jam

mud

net

jog   mix   yuk   vet   zip

Read all the words. Then find the stickers to finish the picture.